HARDPRESS.NET
HOME OF HARD-TO-FIND BOOKS

Thoughts on Such Penal Religious Statutes as Affect the Protestant Dissenters
by William Parry

Address:
HardPress
8345 NW 66TH ST #2561
MIAMI FL 33166-2626
USA
Email: info@hardpress.net

THOUGHTS

ON SUCH

PENAL RELIGIOUS STATUTES

AS AFFECT THE

PROTESTANT DISSENTERS;

Most respectfully submitted to the Consideration of the

HONOURABLE PROMOTERS OF THE BILL

IN FAVOUR OF

PROTESTING ROMAN CATHOLICS.

By WILLIAM PARRY.

LONDON:

PRINTED FOR J. JOHNSON, NO. 72, ST. PAUL'S
CHURCH-YARD.

M,DCC,XCI.

Price ONE SHILLING.

CONTENTS.

T H O U G H T S

o n

Penal Religious Statutes, &c.

SECTION I.

THE wisdom of the present Parliament hath thought proper to introduce a Bill in favour of protesting Roman Catholics; a measure in which both sides of the House are united, and in which every *consistent* friend to toleration will rejoice. When an alteration, so favourable to liberty, is made *in the Constitution*, and relief is granted to one description of subjects, who have long been proscribed and oppressed, it may not be improper to submit to the consideration of the Honourable promoters of the Catholic Bill, and of the Public, an examination of the Penal Statutes which are still in force against another description of British subjects, the Protestant Dissenters, and the propriety of *their* repeal. Candid and impartial men, however divided in their political or religious sentiments, will not

be

be difpleafed at fuch an examination, if con-
ducted with moderation and decorum, on the
principles of truth and juftice, and with that
deference and refpect which are due to Legifla-
tive authority.

The appearances of things are often fallacious,
and lead men to conclufions, which have no
foundation in facts. Under the *mild aufpices* of
the Houfe of Brunfwick, and through the lenient fpirit which has prevailed in the prefent
century, Proteftant Diffenters have *actually* enjoyed a large degree of religious liberty. The
execution of thofe perfecuting laws, by which
their anceftors were haraffed, has grown obfolete, and their enjoyment of liberty has been
nearly as undifturbed and complete as if fuch
laws *had been* repealed. This *actual liberty* has
deceived many *amongft them* into an opinion,
that, as to religion, they were under no re-
ftraints; and has led *others* to conclude haftily,
that Proteftant Diffenters enjoyed a *legal* and
full Toleration. But it will be found on examination, notwithftanding the mildnefs of Government, of which Proteftant Diffenters enter-
tain a grateful fenfe, that many *grievous* and
perfecuting ftatutes are ftill in full force againft
them, from which many amongft them have no
legal relief by the Act of Toleration paffed in
the reign of William III. or the revival of it
in the *prefent* reign.

It is painful to a generous mind, becaufe it is degrading to human nature to recall the imperfections of former times, or drag into public view thofe meafures which had their origin in the mifguided zeal and prejudices, the ignorance and bigotry, or the barbarifm and intolerance of our anceftors. Neverthelefs, fuch an attempt may be ufeful, as it may fhew the expedience of a general revifal of all the penal laws refpecting religion, and of *extirpating* them as a *national difgrace*, from the Statute Book.

By a claufe in the act of Toleration, every Proteftant Diffenter is required, at a General Seffions of the Peace, held for the county or place where he lives, to take the oaths of allegiance and fupremacy, and fubfcribe the declaration againft popery, *to entitle him to the benefit* of the faid act. Many Proteftant Diffenters are unacquainted with this claufe ; and, however it might be obferved near the time when the act paffed, a compliance with it has not been *impofed*, and is generally neglected. Were the obfervance of it to be revived, it would create immenfe trouble to the Juftices of the Peace, if every Diffenter throughout England were to certify his diffent at a Quarter Seffions, and oblige the Court to regifter, and give a certificate of the fame, according to the ftatute. Yet, every Proteftant Diffenter who is not *fo regiftered* is not *legally* tolerated. The liberty

he

he poffeffes, is only by *connivance*, and he is ftill, *in law*, expofed to the ftatutes againft Nonconformity. It is true, that upon compliance with the above claufe in the act of Toleration, all procefs againft him under the penal laws would be ftopped, yet much trouble and vexation might be previoufly caufed by them.

How oppreffive and fevere our penal religious ftatutes are, will appear by a brief ftatement of them, from any of the law books. Unregifted *Lay* Diffenters are liable, according to Burn, to the following penalties for their nonconformity, which might be the occafion of much diftrefs, if any change fhould ever take place in the temper of the times, favourable to perfecution. By the 1 of Eliz. c. 2. f. 14. Every perfon not having reafonable excufe, fhall refort to their parifh church or chapel, or fome other place where common prayer fhall be ufed, on *every* Sunday and holiday, on pain of punifhment by the cenfures of the church, or of forfeiting for every offence 12d. The forfeiture to be levied by the churchwardens. By the 23 of Eliz. c. 1. Every perfon above the age of fixteen years, who fhall not repair to fome church or chapel, or ufual place of common prayer, fhall forfeit for every month TWENTY POUNDS. And if he fhall forbear for twelve months, he fhall be bound to his good behaviour till he conform. By the 29 of Eliz. c. 6. Every offender in not

repairing

repairing to church, having been once convicted, shall, without any other indictment or conviction, pay half-yearly into the Exchequer TWENTY POUNDS for *every month* afterwards, until he conform ; which if he omit to do, the King may seize *all* his goods, and *two* parts of his lands. And by the 3 of J. c. 4. The King may refuse the twenty pounds a month, and take two parts of the land, at his option. By the same statute, churchwardens neglecting to present at the sessions once a year, the monthly absence of *all recusants*, and the names and ages of their children and servants, are liable to a penalty of twenty pounds. By the 3 of J. c. 5. No recusant in not repairing to church, being convicted thereof, shall enjoy any public office, or shall practise law or physic, or be executor, administrator, or guardian. By the 35 of Eliz. c. 1. If any person refusing to repair to church, shall be present at any assembly, meeting, or conventicle, under pretence of any exercise of religion, he shall be *imprisoned* till he conform ; and if he shall not conform in three months, he shall abjure the realm ; which if he shall refuse to do, or after abjuration shall not go, or shall return without licence, he shall be guilty of *felony* without benefit of clergy. And whether he shall abjure or not, he shall forfeit his goods, and shall forfeit his lands

B 3   during

during life. And by the 22 Ch. II. c. 1. If any person being sixteen years of age, shall be present at any conventicle or meeting, under pretence of any exercise of religion, in other manner than according to the liturgy and practice of the church of England, at which there shall be five persons or more assembled, besides those of the houshold, if it be in an house where there is a family ; or if it be in a house, *field*, or place where there is no family, is liable to a fine of five shillings for the first offence, and for every other offence ten shillings, to be levied by distress. Justices of the Peace neglecting to execute this act are subject to a penalty of 100l. and are impowered to enter by force any place where such meetings are held, and even to call the military to their assistance. Every person suffering such meeting in his dwelling-house, or in any of his out-houses, forfeits twenty pounds. And the 13 sec. of this statute directs, that the act shall be construed most *largely* and *beneficially,* for the *suppressing* of conventicles, &c. and no proceedings thereupon are to be *impeached for want of form. Upon this ground,* conviction was affirmed about four years since, against S. Hall, of Heckington, in the county of Lincoln, who had been previously convicted, before Richard Brown, Esq. in the penalty of twenty pounds, under the Conventicle Act, for

a meeta meeting held in his house on the 2d of March, 1786.

The laity amongst Protestant Dissenters are also deprived of *eligibility* to office by the Corporation and Test Acts, and are liable, should they accept them, to dreadful penalties. This subject has undergone such *ample* discussion, that nothing need be here said concerning it, unless it be, that the reasons which may be brought against penal *religious* statutes, apply in their *full force* to those acts, because by them good citizens are deprived of some of the common rights of subjects, *merely* on account of *their religion.*

The obsolete penal laws against Protestant Dissenting Ministers, are not less severe than those which affect the laity. By the 17 of Ch. II. c. 2. No person who shall take upon him to preach in any meeting or conventicle, shall, unless only in passing upon the road, or unless required by any legal process, come within five miles of a city, town corporate, or borough, without taking an oath of allegiance therein mentioned, on pain of 40l. and two justices, on oath of the offence, may commit him for six months. By the 22 of Ch. II. c. 1. If any person shall take upon him to preach or teach in any meeting or conventicle, in other manner than according to the practice of the church of

B 4 England,

England, he fhall forfeit for the firft offence 2ol. and for every other offence 4ol. In cafe he be a ftrangor, or unable to pay, thofe fums may be levied on the goods of *any* perfon prefent. And by the 13 & 14 of Ch. II. c. 4. f. 14. No perfon fhall prefume to confecrate and adminifter the facrament, before he be ordained prieft, according to the form and manner of the church of England, on pain of 1ool. By the 19 of Geo. III. c. 44. Every Proteftant Diffenting Minifter is exempted from the penalties of thefe ftatutes, *who fhall*, at a Quarter Seffions, take the oaths of allegiance and fupremacy, and make and fubfcribe the declaration contained in the faid act. Proteftant Diffenting Minifters have no objection to take the oath of allegiance, or give any other reafonable fecurity, for their fidelity to the ftate. There are, however, difficulties of another nature, which prevent a very large number of them from qualifying according to the late act, whereby they are kept from the enjoyment of *legal* liberty, which the *goodnefs* of the Legiflature intended by that act to afford them.

The form of the oath of *fupremacy* is inconfiftent with the *prefent* ftate of the laws refpecting *popery*. And it is worthy of particular confideration, whether *any Proteftant*, be he a Diffenter or a Conformift, can *now* take that oath con-

confiftently with *truth* and a good confcience. In its prefent form, the perfon taking it folemnly fwears, that " No foreign prince, perfon, pre- " late, ftate, or potentate, *hath*, or ought to " have, any jurifdiction, power, fuperiority, " pre-eminence, or authority, ecclefiaftical or " *fpiritual*, within this realm." The claufe, " *Hath* or ought to have," is evidently intended to declare, that the Pope, neither *hath in fact*, nor ought to have *in right*, any fuch power or authority. But is it not a *fact*, that the fpiritual authority of the Pope is now exercifed refpecting the Roman Catholics in England? Is not that exercife of his fpiritual authority allowed, and even *recognifed*, as to *them*, by the late alterations of the laws in their favour? Are they not protected, in an open acknowledgment to *his* fpiritual authority, while they reject his temporal power? And does not the oath of fupremacy therefore, in denying that he *hath* any fpiritual authority in the realm, affert what is *now* falfe? To many perfons this appears to be the cafe. Would it not then become the wifdom of the Legiflature to new model the oath of fupremacy, in conformity to the *prefent ftate* of the laws relating to popery?

But Proteftant Diffenting Minifters have more ferious difficulties than that now ftated, which prevent them from complying with the

prefent

present terms of Toleration. They consider the qualification required *as implying* an acknowledgment of the *right* of civil governors to interfere in matters of religion and conscience, and to prescribe who shall, or shall not, instruct their fellow-creatures in the principles and duties of the Christian religion. The acknowledgment of such a right they consider as a denial of their great and leading principle, that Jesus Christ possesses the *supreme* and *sole* authority in his church. This principle is the foundation of their dissent. They consider his kingdom as not of a worldly nature; and if they acknowledge a right in the powers of this world, to rule in the affairs of *his* kingdom, they *give up the ground* on which their whole nonconformity is built, and forfeit, as they apprehend, their fidelity and allegiance to HIM whom they own as their *only spiritual* Legislator. This difficulty in the way of qualifying, however it may appear to others, is in their view *great* and *important.* Many of them, therefore, remain unqualified, and consequently are obnoxious to the old penal laws.

Such a difficulty does not indeed affect those who qualify only as Protestant Dissenting *Schoolmasters.* Yet they may be now prevented, by the scruple before stated, as to the oath of supremacy. Every unqualified Dissenting Schoolmaster

mafter is liable, by 23 of Eliz. c. 1. to forfeit 10l. a month, and be imprifoned a year, to 40l. penalty by the 17 C. II. c. 2. and to three months imprifonment, and a forfeiture of 5l. for the fecond and every other offence, by the 13 and 14 Ch. II. c. 4. In addition to thefe penal laws it fhould not be forgotten, that every perfon, whether a Diffenter or of the Eftablifhment, who denies and oppofes, by fpeaking or writing, the doctrine of the Trinity, is, by the 9 and 10 of William the Third, rendered incapable of any office, ecclefiaftical, civil, or military ; difabled from being plaintiff, guardian, executor, or adminiftrator, and from taking any legacy, and liable to *three years* imprifonment !

Such are the principal penal ftatutes in matters of religion ftill in force, and by which Proteftant Diffenters are, at leaft, *liable* to be aggrieved. If the *nature* and *tendency* of *fuch laws* be examined on the principles of reafon, humanity, juftice, religion, and found policy, it will probably be found, that the *repeal* of them is, on all thefe grounds, expedient for the *public* good, and our national honour.

S E C T. II.

WITHOUT entering at large into the arguments for Toleration, which have been fo often urged by its able advocates, a few confiderations

tions will evince, that laws, intended to *force* conscience, and *compel* men to a conformity with the established religion of a state, are contrary to the dictates of *reason*. If there be a *right* belonging to man, either in his *natural* or *social* capacity, which above all others is *essential* and *unalienable*, it is that of *private judgment*. It arises from the very constitution of his nature, as a rational and accountable creature, and is *inseparable* from it. Every man *feels* that he possesses it, and cannot divest himself of it if he would. If he thinks at all, he cannot avoid believing what appears to him to be true, whether it may accord with the judgment of others or not. The human mind is so formed, as to be convinced by evidence and arguments, and cannot receive a conviction of truth by any other means. How absurd the attempt, therefore, *authoritatively to impose* upon it articles of faith, or rites of worship? Men's views in religion, as well as in other matters, are influenced, and in a great degree formed by the circumstances in which they are placed, their education, modes of life, the books they read, and the company with which they converse. In a great nation *these* must be infinitely diversified— and a great *diversity* of sentiment must be the necessary effect. To what end then shall a government dictate to the whole nation what they shall

shall believe, and practise in religion ; or subject any to pains and penalties, if, upon enquiring for themselves, their religious opinions and practices should happen to differ from the public standard. Fines and imprisonments may destroy the *virtuous*, and make hypocrites of the *unprincipled*, but they cannot enlighten the judgment, convince the conscience, or amend the heart.

If uniformity of faith and worship, amongst all the inhabitants of a kingdom, were desirable, the acquisition of this object should be sought by means more rational, and better suited to the nature of the human mind than penal laws can be. If men wish to convince others on any subject, reason dictates that they should *argue*, state the propositions, produce evidences in support of them, present these to the view of their minds, persuade them to attend to the evidence, to exercise their own understanding, and judge for themselves. But it *does not* dictate, that we should impoverish their pockets to enrich their understandings, or confine their bodies in prison, to set them at liberty from the prejudices of their minds. If a member of the Romish church really thinks that the Pope, adorned with his triple-crown, and arrayed in all his pontifical robes, looks *exactly* like Simon Peter in his fisher's coat, a Protestant may pity him

for

for the unhappy prejudices of his education, and, confiftently with reafon and benevolence, may endeavour, by argument, to convince him there is no refemblance between them. But, if this method fails, why fhould he perfecute the Roman Catholic? He will not fee more clearly in a *prifon*, nor will the *darknefs* of a dungeon enable him to diftinguifh betwixt the *dignified* Pontiff and the *humble* Apoftle. In like manner, if a Proteftant Diffenter really cannot find diocefan bifhops and archbifhops, archdeacons, deans, prebendaries, and canons, confiftorial courts, lay-chancellors, and all the forms, articles, and ceremonies of the church of England, *in his New Teftament*, why fhould he, on that account, be made the prey of *rapacious* informers and *fanguinary* laws? Why fhould he be liable to have his goods confifcated, and his perfon torn from all his focial connections, for the ftrength or the weaknefs of his mind? "He has wronged no man, he has "corrupted no man, he has defrauded no man." Would it not be more confiftent with his nature, as a reafonable being, and more *honourable* to religion, to fhew him the parts of the *New Teftament* where thefe things are to be found, or endeavour, by juft reafoning, to convince him, that they are all deducible from it, and fupported by it. If fuch means be not at hand,

hand, or fhould fail to produce a change in his
fentiments, he muft be given up as an incorri-
gible fchifmatic, for the laws againft nonconformity, although they might deprive fociety of an
ufeful member, and the Crown of a *loyal* fubject,
would never make him a *fincere* convert.—Reafon then condemns fanguinary ftatutes, to enforce national uniformity in religion as *abfurd
means*, ill adapted to promote an end which
could *never* be accomplifhed. Yet at the fhrine
of this idol, *uniformity* of *faith and worfhip*,
were offered up the peace and happinefs of thefe
kingdoms for near two centuries! The attempt
of bringing to pafs fuch uniformity, has, indeed,
long ago been given up; why then fhould not
the laws, which brought hecatombs to the altar
of this fair idol, be repealed.

S E C T. III.

PENAL STATUTES, in matters of religion, can
no more be reconciled with the principles of *humanity* than of reafon. Humanity is that *amiable* difpofition of the heart which inclines us to
prevent, commiferate, and relieve the woes of
others, and binds man to his fellow-man. Humanity in individuals forbids them, unlefs on a
very neceffary and unavoidable occafion, to caufe
pain or diftrefs to a fellow-creature. Humanity
in ftates requires, that the code of criminal law

I be

be as lenient, as may confift with the fafety and good order of civil fociety. How repugnant then to *humanity* muft be fuch laws, as render *peaceable* and orderly fubjects of the ftate liable to pains and penalties, merely for their religious opinions ? How inconfiftent is it with this bright ornament of our nature, to deprive *ufeful* and *virtuous* citizens of the common rights of fubjects, or expofe them to want, famine, and the horrors of imprifonment, for no other rea- fon than becaufe they fincerely worfhip the be- nevolent Parent of the univerfe, in that way which they think to be *moft acceptable* to him.

If the tear-fraught eye of humanity could behold the *fcenes of mifery*, which *have been* caufed by our penal religious ftatutes, how *greatly* would fhe be fhocked ? Look into that damp and dreary cell, through the narrow chink, which admits a few fcanty rays of light, to ren- der vifible to the wretched his abode of woe. Behold, by the glimmering of that feeble lamp, a prifoner, *pale* and *emaciated*, feated on the humid earth, and purfuing his daily tafk, to earn the morfel which prolongs his exiftence and confinement together. Near him, reclined in penfive fadnefs, lies a *blind* daughter, compelled to eat the bread of affliction, from the hard earning of an imprifoned father! Paternal af- fection binds her to his heart, and filial gratitude has

has long made her the *daily* companion of his captivity. No other folace remains to him, fave the *mournful one* arifing from the occafional vifits of five other diftreffed children, and an affectionate wife, whom pinching want and grief have worn down to the gate of death. More than ten fummer's funs have rolled over the ftone-roofed manfion of his mifery, whofe reviving rays have never *once penetrated* his fad abode. " Seafons return," but not to *him* returns the cheering light of day, the fmiling bloom of fpring, or found of human joy ! Unfortunate captive ! What is his guilt, what his crimes ? Is he a traitor, or a parricide ? A lewd adulterer, or a vile incendiary ? No, he is *a chriftian fufferer !* Under all his calamities peace reigns in his breaft, heavenly hope gliftens in his eye, and patience fits throned on his *pallid* cheek. He is none other than honeft John Bunyan, languifhing through the *twelfth* year of his imprifonment in Bedford jail, for teaching plain country people the *knowledge* of the fcriptures, and the *practice of virtue !!!*——— It requires the *energy* of Fox, the *eloquence* of Burke, and the *pathos* of Sheridan, to paint the effect of fuch a fcene on the feelings of HUMANITY : My feeble pen drops from the tafk, and leaves *fenfibility* to *endure* thofe fenfations of

C   com-

compaffion and forrow, which it fails to de-
fcribe.

Such, however, were the fcenes which *actually* took place in this land of liberty in the
laft century; and, if they have not been repeated
in the prefent, it is not becaufe the fanguinary
ftatutes which were the caufe of them are repealed, but owing to the milder genius of the
prefent government, and the liberal fpirit of the
times, which have *fufpended* their execution.
Why fhould not the fame caufes operate farther,
to their *repeal?*

Motives of *humanity*, as well as others, might
induce the Legiflature to adopt fuch a meafure.
Great as is the *actual* liberty of Diffenters, it
has not a *legal* fecurity; and, mild as is the *prefent* Government, there is no certainty that every
future Prince, or *future* Adminiftration, will
be equally tolerant. What has taken place,
may revolve, and occur again, in the courfe of
human affairs. Future times may fee future
ftatefmen, and bifhops of the fame temper and
fpirit as Clarendon, Sheldon, and Gunning
were, in the laft age. Is it then *too great a boon*
for the humanity of the Legiflature to fecure
to the Proteftant Diffenters that religious liberty which it has long fuffered them to enjoy
by *connivance*, and relieve *them* from that anxiety
which cannot be wholly removed while the

2   penal

penal ftatutes againft them are continued in force? Or, has the conduct of *Proteftant* Diffenters towards the prefent Government, and reigning Family, poffeffed *no* merit, which may be thought to entitle them to fuch a grant, at a feafon when farther relief and toleration are given to the Roman Catholics?

S E C T. IV.

IF, however, humanity did not operate in favour of fuch a repeal, the *higher* claims of JUSTICE would. The exiftence and perpetuity of penal ftatutes refpecting religion, are inconfiftent with *juftice*. Religion being a *perfonal* concern, *juftice* requires, that every man fhould be left at full liberty to judge for himfelf refpecting it. Nothing upon earth is *infallible*, except the fcriptures. It is at leaft *poffible*, that men may be mifled by national creeds, and public formularies, as much as by private fpeculations. Yet every man muft *perfonally* abide the *eternal* confequences of his religion, whether it be good or bad, falfe or true. In a matter of fuch *vaft*, and *endlefs* importance, he ought then to be left *free* to exercife his underftanding and confcience in the beft manner that he is able. Human authority and power ought not to *impofe*, or have any influence *here*; be-

caufe

cause it is impossible that they should be answerable to *individuals* for the consequences. Every man, therefore, should be permitted to examine and judge for himself, and seek his salvation, in that way which appears to him right. But penal religious statutes tend to deprive men of the right of private judgment, *fetter* and *cramp* them in the exercise of it, and *punish* them on that account. They are, therefore, evidently *inconsistent* with the *most obvious* dictates of justice.

The obligations of this immutable rule of action requires, that men should not *injure* the rights of others, in the exercise of what *they apprehend* to be their own rights. If, therefore, the government of any state, supported in the measure by the *majority* of the people, thinks proper to *establish* any form of religion, it ought to be with *full liberty of dissent*, to those who do not approve of it. For, to *oblige* men to conform to the religion of a state, against the dictates of their consciences, or subject them to legal incapacities and punishments for their non-conformity, is to take away from them the *first* and *dearest* of all their rights, that of *private judgment*. Yet, on this unrighteous basis, stand all the obsolete laws against non-conformity. An ecclesiastical establishment therefore, *without a toleration*, must, in all cases, be an

establish-

eſtabliſhment of *ecclefiaſtical tyranny*. And as juſtice requires toleration, ſo it ought to be *full* and *complete* toleration ; for, in proportion as it is partial and defective, in the ſame degree the legiſlative ſyſtem *infringes* on the *unalienable rights* of men, and *departs* from the *eternal* obligations of juſtice.

JUSTICE requires, that men who are guilty of *no crime, ſhould not* be made ſubject to *puniſhment*. But, to think and act for themſelves in matters of religion, if it be not meritorious, is certainly in itſelf *no crime*. It is true, that the exerciſe of private judgment in religious concerns, may be, and often has been decreed *criminal, by human laws*. But the laws of men cannot alter the *nature of moral actions*, or make that to be *wrong* which is in itſelf *eſſentially right*, or that to be *right* which is in itſelf *eſſentially wrong*. Much as we have heard of the *omnipotence* of Parliaments, and *ſupreme* as their legiſlative authority, in all things which reſpect the ſafety and government of *civil* ſociety *ought* to be, they neither poſſeſs, nor have ever claimed, a power of altering *moral* obligations. Morality and juſtice are things, in their own nature, *eternal* and *unalterable*, and cannot be changed by the vote of any aſſembly upon earth, however ſage and venerable. If it be *not criminal*, therefore, that men ſhould judge for themſelves

C 3

ſelves

selves in things which respect their souls and their salvation, laws which would punish them for the exercise of their *private judgment*, must be most manifestly *unjust*. And such are all the penal laws against non-conformity. They were enacted to punish men for that which is *confessedly* no crime, which is indeed the *first* prerogative of human nature! However ancient therefore such laws may be, or however wrought into the English constitution, justice demands that they should be repealed, and cast out of it, as parts which never were its *ornaments*, and have long been its *disgrace*.

Justice requires, that men should not be punished for their opinions or sentiments, but for their *criminal actions* only. The overt acts of men are the *only* proper objects of criminal law; and if laws are made to punish them for bad opinions or intentions, before they appear in overt acts, against the *peace* of society, a door is opened to every species of persecution and oppression. To think differently from established creeds, to speak and write in support of private religious opinions, or assemble in a peaceable manner, and worship God, otherwise than according to prescribed forms, are not overt acts against the *peace* or *well-being* of society. For, although by the alchymy of penal laws, and the rhetoric of indictments,
such

such actions may have been changed into crimes, and construed into attempts, *vi et armis*, against the *peace* of our Sovereign Lord the King, yet nothing can be plainer to the common sense of mankind, than that *these* are *innocent actions*, which no way *disturb* or *injure* the peace of society. Accordingly, they are now, under *certain conditions*, allowed and permitted, by the act of Toleration. Yet, the whole artillery of penal religious statutes is levelled against men's opinions, and directed and designed to punish them, either for their sentiments and intentions *only*, or for such actions as are in themselves *innocent* and *just*.——Such reasoning as shews that men ought not to be punished by *preventive* laws, or for any thing but overt acts, applies, undoubtedly, to the case of the Roman Catholics, as well as that of *Protestant* Dissenters, and shews, that the whole system of laws against them has proceeded upon an unjustifiable principle. Accordingly, it has been heard respecting *them*, by the Legislature, and the laws altered in their favour. Why should not similar alterations be made respecting *Protestant* Dissenters ?

JUSTICE farther requires, that in all cases of criminal process, the punishment should be *proportioned* to the offence. But, what *just* proportion is there, between heavy fines, confisca-

tion

tion of goods, and imprifonment, and the *harm-
lefs* action of worfhipping God, according to
the dictates of a man's confcience ? Many actions, which have a pernicious influence on fociety, have no punifhment affixed to them, in
our code of criminal law; while *this*, which
tends to make a man a *more virtuous* citizen,
has fuch *fevere* penalties annexed to it, by the
old religious ftatutes. If a company of Bac-
chanalians affemble to offer copious libations
to the god of wine, and mix their orgies with
fuch *lewd* and *profane* converfation, as mutually
contaminates their minds, confirms them in
vice, and fends them from their nocturnal revels,
fit only to *pollute* and *injure* mankind, no punifhment, *adequate* to the *ill confequences* of *fuch*
actions to fociety, is provided by our laws.
But, if more than five fober chriftians, above
fixteen years of age, fhould affemble at a neigh-
bour's houfe, which was not licenfed as a place
of worfhip, fhould fpend the evening in *rational*
converfation, on moral and religious fubjects,
conclude their meeting with an extemporary
prayer delivered by one of them, for the favour
of Heaven on themfelves, their *King*, their
country, and all mankind, and go away with
their hearts confirmed in every moral and virtuous difpofition, to *improve* and *blefs* fociety, by
their good conduct and example; *this*, in the eye
of

of our criminal law, would be *iniquity punishable by the Judge*; and the parties would *now* be liable to the penalties of the Conventicle Act. Can *this* be JUST ? Is this a law fit to exist in a *Christian* country ? Can laws, formed upon such principles, be worthy of *preservation ?* Ought they not rather to be repealed, for the credit of *public justice,* and the *honour* of our national character ?

S E C T. V.

IF penal religious statutes are, as above represented, inconsistent with the *plainest maxims* of justice, how must they appear, when examined on the principles of religion, and compared with the *benevolent* spirit of Christianity ? By Christianity is not here intended *any* human establishments of it, but pure Christianity, as it is delineated in the writings of the New Testament. Blended with human corruptions, and confounded and lost amongst the prejudices and superstitions of mankind, its *native* benevolence and glory have been *often* obscured ; and something, under the *same name,* but of a *different* genius, *ferocious* and *cruel* in aspect, and *formidable* in power, has long ago stalked forth, and spread devastation and terror amidst the nations of the earth. But *pure* Christianity, as it appears in the discourses of Jesus Christ, and in the

the preaching and writings of his Apoſtles, wears
the moſt *mild* and *amiable* features. Its genius
and ſpirit are ſuited to the qualities of the human mind, calculated to enlighten, convince,
and reclaim mankind. It is deſigned to lead
men, through the knowledge of Divine truth, to
the enjoyment of peace and hope, and the practice of the moſt *pure* morality, and *ſublime* virtue. For this purpoſe it ſtates propoſitions and
arguments, preſents the evidence of truth to
our minds, and commands us to believe and
obey, not on the *credit* of *human* authority, or
through the *terror* of *human* laws, but upon the
moſt rational, convincing, and certain of all evidence, the *teſtimony* of God. By ſuch means it
was at firſt propagated by the Apoſtles of
Chriſt. *They* had no penal ſtatutes to *force* con-
ſcience. They uſed no temporal puniſhments
to *oblige* men to embrace their doctrine. They
had not the aid of human power to ſpread the
goſpel of Jeſus Chriſt. Nor did they need
ſuch *unſuitable* and *ineffectual* means. *The weapons
of their warfare were not carnal, but mighty
through God.* Enriched with the knowledge of
truth, and attended with the power of working
miracles, as a Divine confirmation of the truth
they taught, they went forth to bear a plain,
faithful, and artleſs teſtimony, to the doctrines
and facts reſpecting Jeſus Chriſt. By ſuch
means,

means, their doctrine had a rapid spread, not only without the assistance of *human* laws, but against the strongest opposition from the powers of this world, and proved victorious over the prejudices, ignorance, idolatry, and vices of mankind. Thus were the first and *most pure* Christian churches formed; and owed their existence and support, not to an *alliance* with human governments, but to the force of *Divine truth*, and the favourable co-operation of Heaven. If, therefore, the true genius of Christianity be compared with that of human establishments of it; or the *primitive* and *apostolic* mode of its propagation, be contrasted with the *means* employed to enforce *national conformity*, how wide and striking must the difference appear? The *former* are all excellent, worthy of God, and suitable and *benevolent* to man; the *latter* inconsistent with his intellectual qualities, *cruel* and *destructive* in their operation, and *dishonourable* to the civil governments and ecclesiastical constitutions, under which they have been used.

As Christianity employs the most proper means of conviction, so it condemns a persecuting and *imposing* spirit, and the exercise of *authority in matters of religion*. When the Disciples of Christ wished for temporal punishment to fall on those who did not receive him, the

bene-

benevolent Saviour told them, *they knew not what spirit they were of*; and assured them, that he came *not to destroy mens lives, but to save them*. He taught his followers, that the most perfect *equality*, and *freedom of enquiry*, should subsist amongst them as *his subjects*, that they were all brethren, and though the kings of the Gentiles *exercised authority*, yet, that so it *should not be among them*. Agreeably to his instructions, the Apostles themselves, as men, disclaimed *authority* over conscience. They did not require persons to surrender up the use of private judgment, or *tamely* submit to their *mandates*, without enquiring for themselves. On the contrary, they declared that they *had not dominion* over the faith of Christians, but were fellow helpers of their joy. How utterly irreconcileable, therefore, with the doctrine of Christ, and the declaration and temper of his Apostles, are laws which *authoritatively* demand assent to *human creeds* and *liturgies*, and punish men for their refusal. However these things may have been found *amongst Christians*, they *cannot* be found in *Christianity itself*, but are contrary to it.

The benevolent *precepts* of the Gospel, and the gentle spirit which it inculcates, equally condemns penal laws in religion. Far from encouraging the smallest degree of persecution,

Chris-

Chriftianity commands its adherents to fhew all *gentlenefs* towards all men, and in meeknefs to *inftruct* thofe who oppofe themfelves. If any who profefs it are overtaken with a fault, it requires his brethren to reftore him, not by temporal *pains* and *penalties*, but in the fpirit of meeknefs. It teaches its followers the *moft pure* benevolence towards *all* mankind, requires them to *love* their enemies, and do *good*, not evil, to them that *hate* them. It commands them to do to others all things, whatfoever they would that others fhould do to them. How incompatible then are the principle and fpirit of all perfecuting religious ftatutes, with the benevolent precepts of the Gofpel? Pure Chriftianity, as it appears in the Scriptures, is a religion of peace and love, defcended from Heaven to inftruct and blefs mankind. It is calculated to unite them in bonds of mutual forbearance, charity, and goodnefs, to eradicate from amongft them all *injuftice* and *oppreffion*, and to dethrone civil and ecclefiaftical tyranny, while it confirms and ftrengthens *reafonable* and *juft* governments. In proportion, therefore, as the genuine *knowledge* and *influence* of it fhall extend, it will extirpate both public and private injuries, improve and purify mankind, and render the world happy. It muft then be fomething very different from the gentle and benevolent fpirit of the Gofpel, which firft

gave

gave rife to *penal* laws in religion; which changed the *pastoral* staff into a *destroying* sword, and the *meek* and *holy* Guides of the Church into *furious* and *bloody* persecutors. . Such laws must have been intended to subserve some *other* cause than that of Jesus Christ, and to promote *other* interests than those of *truth* and *virtue*. *These*, indeed, could never be promoted by them. They are means which the truth and precepts of the Gospel condemn, and which Christian virtue abhors. Surely it is time, that Christians in every nation should unite in seeking, by peaceable methods, the abolition of persecuting laws and edicts, and join their efforts to roll away the reproach, which their existence has long affixed to the Christian name!

S E C T. VI.

CONSIDERATIONS of *policy*, as well as religion, may evince the impropriety of penal religious statutes, and the necessity of their repeal. Political considerations generally have their full weight with Statesmen and Legislators, and ought, undoubtedly, to be regarded, so far as they are consistent with the stronger obligations of justice and goodness. In the present case, they unite with *those*, to strengthen the argument against the penal laws. One of the *first* and

chief

chief objects of civil policy, is to afford *personal safety* and *protection* to peaceable and virtuous citizens, whose industry and commerce, trade and manufactures, add to the strength and riches of the country. But penal statutes in religion, instead of affording *security*, tend to *harass* and *distress* virtuous citizens. Instead of protecting and encouraging them, they are calculated to drive them into other nations and countries, where they may enjoy liberty of conscience without disturbance. To the present time France has felt *baneful effects*, and England and Holland have reaped *great* and *solid advantages* from the revocation of the Edict of Nantz. It is a branch of *good policy*, therefore, to countenance Toleration in its *full* extent, because it operates *to promote* trade and commerce, arts and manufactures, the *resources* of taxation, and of *national* force, safety, and honour. Whatever may be men's sentiments in religion, their diligence and exertions in commerce are a public advantage. However false may be their creed, their *cash* is sterling, and a wise Statesman, though he may not regard their opinions, should regard their quota of the taxes, and protect them for the sake of the *latter*, if not of the former.

To *strengthen Government*, is another important object of civil policy. Factions, in proportion to their number and influence, weaken and

embarrass

embarrafs Governments, clog their operations, and leffen their refpectability and fecurity. Every wife Statefman will endeavour, therefore, to prevent or break factions, and aim to render the Government both *firm* and *refpectable*. For this purpofe, he will adopt meafures which tend to conciliate the *affections* and *efteem* of the nation, weaken the prejudices of parties, and render the Government, if poffible, beloved by all orders and defcriptions of men. No *fingle meafure*, perhaps, will produce thefe effects in fo great a degree, as a *full* and *legal* Toleration. The hiftory of mankind proves, that men are more tenacious of their *religious* than of their *civil* rights, provided they are both *equally* underftood; and they will be ready to overlook many imperfections in a Government, which allows them the full enjoyment of the rights of confcience. But, in any ftate, laws which *profcribe* and *perfecute* all but the adherents of the *eftablifhed* religion, muft tend, according as their operation is felt, to alienate the affections of all who fuffer by them from the Government, to fow the feeds of animofity and variance amongft the people, to give the different and jarring fectaries one common bond of union, and difpofe them, when opportunity offers, to join in a change. An impartial obferver may fee, that the troubles in the reign of Charles the Firft

had

had their origin in the *persecuting laws* of Queen Elizabeth, as well as in the high notions of the prerogative on which that unfortunate Prince endeavoured to act. What injurious effects also were produced, by the persecution of the Dissenters in the reign of Charles the Second? How much disaffection to the Government arose from them? What animosities and party zeal did they cause amongst the people, the remains of which, unhappily, are not eradicated to the present day? But if there are *no penal* religious statutes existing in a state, one great cause of disaffection is removed. However numerous may be the sects, or religious parties in it, none of them will give the Government the least disturbance. Enjoying full religious liberty, each person will *naturally* attend to his own particular concerns, and the nation will be *peaceable* and *happy*. Has not *this been*, in a great degree, the case in this country since the Revolution, through the *actual* liberty which has been enjoyed? Would it not then be *wise policy*, to *legalize* that liberty which has already, while possessed by *sufferance*, been productive of such happy consequences?

To increase *national happiness*, is a third important end of civil policy. The happiness of the public, circumstances of war or peace, commerce, riches, and civil constitution, being supposed the

D   same,

fame, will ever be in proportion to their *virtue*. Whatever tends to promote *virtue*, tends, in the fame degree, to promote *happinefs*. But Toleration has an eminent tendence to improve public virtue, and confequently happinefs. Befides the fcope which it gives to the abilities of men of every denomination of Chriftians, to promote the interefts of *morality*, and in *this*, furely, they are all agreed, it creates a *ftimulus* which operates powerfully on the eftablifhed Clergy. Without a Toleration, an eftablifhed Clergy, fecure in the enjoyment of emoluments and honours, would relax in their *zeal* and *induftry* to *inftruct* the people, become *vicious* themfelves, and render others fo by their negligence and example. This is a natural effect of *riches* and *fecurity* on human nature, and perhaps to this, as well as other caufes, were owing the general profligacy, ignorance, and neglect of their duties, fo notorious in the Romifh Clergy before the Reformation. An oppofition of interefts creates emulation. And while there are numerous Diffenters of different denominations, aiming to inftruct multitudes in Chriftian knowledge and practice, although all amongft the Clergy may not be influenced by fuch a fact, yet many, undoubtedly, will be excited by it, to a better difcharge of their duty. Thus fentiments favourable to virtue will be more diffufed,

fufed, the people in general will receive more inftruction, and as they become more *virtuous*, will be more *happy*. Is it not then found policy to repeal laws, which, if they had their *full* operation, would not only diftrefs and punifh honeft, unoffending, and ufeful citizens, but make the Clergy *indolent*, and the people *vicious ?*

But it may be afked, if *civil* policy does not countenance the perfecuting ftatutes; does not *ecclefiaftical* policy juftify their exiftence, and require that they be perpetuated ? To this it may be anfwered in the firft place, that fuch an objection cannot be urged by the friends of the Englifh eftablifhment, without *yielding at once* the palm of victory, to the arguments of *Proteftant* Diffenters on the fubjects of Church-government, and the nature of the kingdom of Chrift. If penal religious ftatutes are neceffary for the *fafety* and *prefervation* of the eftablifhment, it muft then be fomething different from *pure* and *undefiled* Chriftianity. The Gofpel of Jefus Chrift is able to ftand on its *own* evidence. His Church, built on the immoveable foundation of Divine truth, and fupported by his providence, defies all oppofition. The powers of earth and hell can never overthrow it, or *endanger* its exiftence. The caufe of God and *truth* needs not the *puny* aid of *human* laws for its defence, and can derive no honour from

D 2

them.

them. To call *their* affiftance to its fupport, is to touch with *unhallowed* hands the ark of God! Every thing in religion muft ftand or fall by arguments drawn from *Scripture* and *reafon*, and to fay, that penal ftatutes are neceffary for the fupport of the Church, is *virtually* to acknowledge, that its form and conftitution *do not ftand* on *this ground,* and that it owes its exiftence and fupport, *not* to its conformity to the *only* rule of faith and practice amongft *Proteftants*, the BIBLE, but to *obfolete* and *fanguinary* Acts of Parliament.

But the objection itfelf is founded upon a miftake: If by meafures of *ecclefiaftical* policy are intended, fuch as conduce to the *fafety* and *refpectability* of the eftablifhed Church, it may be clearly proved, that the penal laws are not neceffary to either of thefe ends. No human eftablifhment of religion can ever become *fafe* or *refpectable* by *intolerant* meafures. *While* it *oppreffes* and *perfecutes,* thofe who *fuffer* by it will be *irritated* to *oppofe* it, not merely by arguments, but by other means, if in their power. This is a natural effect of *oppreffion* on the human mind; it provokes refiftance. Such refiftance was *formerly* made againft the Englifh eftablifhment, in confequence of its *oppreffive* meafures. Its own *intolerance* raifed that ftorm which overturned it in the laft century, and the Church

Church NEVER WAS SAFE, UNTIL THE PERSECU-
TION OF THE DISSENTERS CEASED. At no period has the Church enjoyed such long and un-
disturbed *repose*, nor possessed such an high degree of *respectability* as through the present century. For *both*, she has been indebted to the act
of Toleration, and that moderate spirit, which
has suspended the *operation* of the penal laws,
even as to those against whom their *legal force*
has been retained. And, other causes remaining
the same, every *human* establishment of religion
will ever be secure and respected, in proportion
as it countenances *Toleration*. No abilities, ta-
lents, or worldly honours, can render *respectable*,
in any nation upon earth, a *band* of persecutors.
But, moderation commands respect, softens prejudices, and buries former animosities in obli-
vion. These happy effects the Church has, in
some measure, felt by her forbearance; but she
will never experience them *fully*, until she exerts
her influence to procure the revocation of such
persecuting statutes, as *formerly* operated to
shake her own foundations, and render her des-
picable in the eyes of the reformed part of
Europe.

If the penal religious statutes be at all necessary for the safety and honour of the Church,
they ought to be executed. What advantage
or glory can she derive from *obsolete* laws, sup-

D 3   posed

poſed to exiſt only on old duſty parchments, and
not brought into *effeĉt*. If they are in themſelves *good*, they ought to be put in force. If
they are *not fit* to be executed, they *ought* to be
repealed. If it be *politic* to retain them, it
muſt be *politic* to execute them. If any *ſolid*
reaſon could be aſſigned to juſtify their *exiſtence*,
it would equally juſtify their *execution*. But it
ſeems to be allowed, that the execution of ſuch
ſtatutes, in the *preſent* day, would create general
diſguſt and abhorrence. Even the moſt zealous
and exalted friends of the eſtabliſhment diſavow
ſuch perſecuting meaſures as they were intended
to create, and aſſure us, that " The moderation
" of the Church of England is her higheſt
" boaſt, and brighteſt ornament." Church policy, as well as other cauſes, has long ſuſpended
the operation of thoſe laws ; why ſhould it not
alſo procure their *repeal?* If it be proper, that
ſuch a degree of *aĉtual* liberty, as has been enjoyed by Proteſtant Diſſenters, ſhould be poſ-
ſeſſed by them, why ſhould it not be made
legal? If it be *politic* that they ſhould *poſſeſs it*,
how can it be *impolitic* to give them a *legal ſe-
curity* for its *poſſeſſion?* To retain perſecuting
laws, *in terrorem*, would only tend to awaken
ſuſpicion in the minds of all *impartial* judges,
that ſuch profeſſions of moderation were not
made with *ſincerity*; and that as the Church
thought

thought proper to *keep* them, she intended, at some fit opportunity, to make *use* of them. True maxims, however, of Church policy, shew, that their retention conduces neither to the *security*, nor to the *honour* of the establishment, and vindicate the sentiment of the great Lord Chatham, that " Sectaries were never injurious " or dangerous, but when they were persecuted " by the ruling church."

S E C T. VII.

IT appears then, that penal statutes in religion, will not bear the examination of reason, humanity, justice, christianity, or true maxims civil, or even ecclesiastical policy. It may therefore be asked, " What has been the origin " of persecution," seeing it cannot be justified on any of these principles, and yet *has* taken place, under all the forms of religion that have been patronised and *established* by civilized states ? An impartial attention to the history of mankind will shew, that the true origin of *this* destructive practice, has always been, an *indiscreet zeal* for human establishments of religion, whether they were Pagan or Christian, Popish or Protestant. Wherever men's *temporal* prosperity, honours, and emoluments, *have been connected* with an *established* religion, they have had *another interest* to support, *separate* from the interest

of

of *truth* and *virtue*, and which they have often
supported by means inconsistent with *both*. This
has been a *common defect*, running through *all*
human religious establishments of every kind.
If idolatry had not been the *established* religion
of the Roman Empire, it would not have persecuted the primitive christians. But the hea-
then priests were solicitous to *crush* the *harmless*
disciples of Jesus, lest the truth they taught,
should, in its influence, destroy their temples,
their idols, and their *gain* together. If Con-
stantine had not made a *civil establishment* of
christianity, he would not have employed persecuting measures against the Pagans. But *interest then* required, that idolatry should be sup-
pressed by force, lest the temples should be
restored, and the *revenues* of the church *impaired*.
If the orthdox and hetrodox, under the following Emperors, had not, each in their turn,
sought the patronage of the state, and endeavoured to *establish* their *own party*, they would
not alternately have persecuted one another.
Zeal for the establishment of their own tenets and
influence, first-lead professing christians to draw
the blood of one another ! The *same cause* continued, in after times, to produce the *same effect*.
If *popery* had not been established through
Europe, the Albigenses, and Valdenses, and
Lollards, would not have been persecuted. A
fear

fear that *their pure* principles and practice, would, in time, weaken the *authority* of the Pope, and leffen the *influence* and *riches* of the priefthood, roufed the thunder of the Vatican, and darted the lightning of ecclefiaftical vengeance, on thefe unhappy fufferers. Not the love of *virtue*, but of *power* and *riches*, kindled the flames of perfecution through Europe. The Marian perfecution here had the fame origin. Not *pure* and *favage cruelty*, but a dread, left the principles of the reformation fhould *regain* their influence in the kingdom, and the power and wealth of the *popifh* clergy be loft, gave birth to thofe fanguinary meafures which brought the *venerable* Latimer, and *an hoft* of other pious witneffes to the ftake. Happy would it have been for the credit of all proteftants, if fimilar caufes had not operated amongft them. But, if epifcopacy had not been eftablifhed, the reign of Elizabeth had not *been difgraced* by the perfecuting laws againft the Puritans ; nor Fox, the learned and laborious martyrologift, been *neglected* to *poverty* and *want*, becaufe of his fcruples as to the habits, while his *acts and monuments* were ordered to be read in the *churches*. If Prefbyterianifm had not been *eftablifhed* by the long Parliament, they would not have perfecuted the adherents of epifcopacy ;

nor

nor would those, who had just emancipated themselves from oppression, have become *immediately, oppressors* in their turn. If the present establishment had not been made under Charles the Second, and uniformity of faith and worship *imposed* upon *all* persons, the sanguinary laws, afterwards made, had not existed ; nor *peaceable* and pious men, been *fined* and *imprisoned, impoverished* and *destroyed,* for worshipping God according to their consciences. In all these cases, not a zeal for *truth,* but zeal for an *establishment,* produced effects, *baneful* and *destructive* to the peace and happiness of mankind, which the faithful pen of history has recorded, to the everlasting infamy of the respective times, and ecclesiastical constitutions, under which they took place. And this *zeal* was *indiscreet* and intemperate. Human establishments of religion, whether in themselves *proper* or *improper,* may be *better* secured by lenient measures, as the history of this country since the Revolution abundantly proves.

May it not be hoped therefore, that such *indiscreet* zeal for their promotion will never be revived, but that the Legislature will concede to *Protestant* Dissenters, a repeal of the penal statutes still in force against them, and the enjoyment of a *full* and *legal* Toleration ? If, in

I   its

its wisdom, the Roman Catholics are thought worthy of farther indulgence, why should not the *Protestant* Dissenters also be so considered. If it be satisfied, that those disaffected principles, which instigated the rebellions against the present reigning family, no longer exist amongst *that* denomination, and of this the Legislature is the proper judge; no doubt, surely, can be entertained of the *fidelity* and *loyalty* of the *Protestant* Dissenters, whose attachment to the House of Hanover was always *unshaken*, and has repeatedly appeared in the most distinguished manner, and on the most *trying* occasions.

It cannot *now* be *consistently* said, that the penal laws respecting Dissenters ought not to be repealed, because they are *essential* parts of the Constitution. No part of the English Constitution used to be considered more *essential* and *sacred* than the laws against *popery*. They were long regarded as the palladium, if not of our liberties, at least of the Protestant religion, and the *Protestant succession*. Yet, it is now thought *just* and *expedient*, in a great degree, to repeal them. If, however, after such a step, *nothing* were to be done in favour of the *Protestant* Dissenters, would it not give the world *just* reason to suspect, that the church was more disposed to favour the Roman Catholics, than her *fellow Pro-*

Proteftants? Or would it indeed be poffible, in *that cafe,* for the moft *unprejudiced* and *impartial* minds, to avoid fuch a conclufion? For the *confiftency* of Government therefore, and the *credit* both of the eftablifhment and the nation, as well as for the *relief* of Diffenters, it is to be wifhed that the Honourable Senators, who have promoted the Catholic Bill, would direct their attention to the laws whereby Proteftant Diffenters either are, or might be aggrieved, and the neceffity of their repeal.

S E C T. VIII.

STILL it may be urged fuch a repeal would be an INNOVATION. But, it ought to be remembered, that at any *former* period, under a Proteftant government, no innovation would have been thought more *dangerous* than the repeal of the *popifh* laws. Yet, in the prefent day, this meafure is judged to be not only fafe, but expedient and proper; and can it be lefs *proper or expedient,* that *full* liberty fhould be granted to *Proteftants?* It ought not to be forgotten alfo, that the penal religious ftatutes were *themfelves innovations,* at the time they were introduced; innovations, which proved a fource of much evil, but never produced any public benefit to the nation! Where then can
be

be the hazard of revoking laws, which have been found so improper and useless, that their execution has been long ago laid aside?

Innovations, certainly, ought not to be made in the laws of a country, upon *trivial* or *flight* occasions, or where no *valuable* end was likely to be attained by them. But, if *no evil* and *much good* may be derived from a measure, why should it be rejected because it is *new*? The world in general, and this nation in particular, is greatly indebted to *innovations*. Since the earth was peopled, every change favourable to *virtue, civilization,* and *happiness,* has been an *innovation.* What great advantages, temporal and eternal, are derived to mankind, from the christian religion? Yet the introduction of *christianity* was an *innovation.* What great benefits do the *present* possessors of the Abbey-lands in this country receive from their fair estates? Yet the Reformation, and the abolition of the Monasteries, to which they are indebted for them, were *innovations.* What invaluable advantages has Great Britain reaped from the expulsion of the house of Stuart, and the accession of the house of Brunswick to the throne? Yet the Revolution, and the introduction of the Hanoverian family, were *innovations.* Every new act of Parliament, and
every

every change in the Adminiftration, is an *inno-vation*. But are new laws never to be made, nor Adminiftrations altered? In fhort, *innovation* may be an *Angel of peace*, to bring joy and happinefs to mankind, or a *Fiend of darknefs*, the harbinger of *mifery* and *defolation*, according, as new meafures adopted, are *beneficial* or *in-jurious*. The *cry of innovation* then, however it may be the plea of the *crafty*, and the fcare-crow of the *timid*, will have no weight in *great* and *wife* minds, who will not fo much regard whether a meafure be *new*, as whether it be JUST and GOOD.

Thefe qualities the repeal of penal religious ftatutes would evidently poffefs. In the courfe of what has been here advanced to prove or illuftrate the neceffity of fuch a repeal, nothing has been faid *defignedly difrefpectful*, nor ought any reflections, contained in the foregoing pages on the Penal Laws, to be confidered as applica-ble to the prefent Governors of the church, inafmuch as they have difclaimed the *intolerant principles* on which they were founded. No-thing remains neceffary, but that their profef-fions of moderation be confirmed by the aboli-tion of thofe laws.

The arguments in favour of *fuch* a meafure, are not the voice of party or intereft, of difguft or or prejudice, but the voice of reason, humanity, and justice, of revealed religion, and sound policy. And that Legislature, which shall first wipe away this national disgrace, and *establish* harmony and peace, by *establishing full* and *complete* religious liberty, will acquire a *degree* of *honour* never yet attained, even by a British Government, and be recorded in the annals of *immortal fame.*

THE END.

ERRATA.

Page 27, line 3, from the bottom, for *authority,* read *human authority.*

Page 28, line 2, from the bottom, for *condemns,* read *condemn.*

Check Out More Titles From HardPress Classics Series In this collection we are offering thousands of classic and hard to find books. This series spans a vast array of subjects – so you are bound to find something of interest to enjoy reading and learning about.

Subjects:
Architecture
Art
Biography & Autobiography
Body, Mind &Spirit
Children & Young Adult
Dramas
Education
Fiction
History
Language Arts & Disciplines
Law
Literary Collections
Music
Poetry
Psychology
Science
…and many more.

Visit us at www.hardpress.net

CPSIA information can be obtained
at www.ICGtesting.com
Printed in the USA
BVHW042331110819
555626BV00017B/4953/P